CW00726490

Cooking for
My Cavy
Recipes for Guinea Pig Treats

Fiction titles by Melissa J. Taylor

Caroline's Cavy Series

Gram, Gramps, and a Guinea Pig Named Rover

The Guinea Pigs' Summer Storybook
The Guinea Pigs' Fall Storybook
The Guinea Pigs' Winter Storybook
The Guinea Pigs' Spring Storybook

Cooking for My Cavy
Recipes for Guinea Pig Treats

by Melissa J. Taylor

Cooking for My Cavy: Recipes for Guinea Pig Treats
Copyright © 2003, 2013 by Melissa J. Taylor

All rights reserved. No part of this book may be reproduced in part or in whole via any means, without the permission of the author.

Cover design and interior illustrations by Melissa J. Taylor

First printing 2003.
Second printing (revised) 2013.

In cases when an illustration appears in The Guinea Pigs' Storybook series, it has been marked as to which book you can find it in. You can read the story, while your piggies eat the complementary treat!

Oven temperatures listed are U.S. (Fahrenheit). Recipes are to be made by adults, or under adult supervision.

Summary: More than twenty-five recipes for creating treats for guinea pigs.

ISBN-13: 978-1494204853
ISBN-10: 1494204851

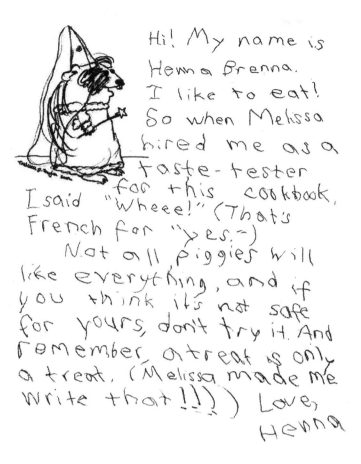

Hi! My name is Henna Brenna. I like to eat! So when Melissa hired me as a taste-tester for this cookbook, I said "Wheee!" (That's French for "yes.")

Not all piggies will like everything, and if you think it's not safe for yours, don't try it. And remember, a treat is only a treat. (Melissa made me write that!!!)) Love, Henna

Remember—treats are *only* treats! Talk to your trusted small animal veterinarian to find out more about what your guinea pig(s) can safely eat, including specific ingredients and quantities.

Illustration from *The Guinea Pigs' Fall Storybook.*

7

Mini Guinea

1 apple
1 carrot
4 raisins

After washing the apple thoroughly, completely remove the skin. Cut the apple in half, and core it. Place each half flat side down on a plate.

Cut a slit in both sides of the front top, and set in small carrot slices to mimic ears.

Make a little hole in the front sides of each apple, and place in raisins for eyes.

Now, you have made one for you—and one for your guinea pigs!

Optional Additions

* Place a baby-cut carrot in front of the mini guinea's "mouth."

* Put a trail of raisins behind the guinea pig. (Time to clean the cage!)

~
Guinea pigs can recognize people's footsteps. Have you ever heard your piggy begging for a treat, when you're not even in the room?
~

Cherry~ Apple Jelly

1/4 cup cherries
1/2 apple (cored, with skin removed)
1 tablespoon water

Remove the stems from the cherries, cut them in half, and remove the pits. Make sure what you have equals 1/4 cup. (It will be around 8 cherries.)

Whirl them in a blender, along with the apple and water.

Place the puree in a microwave-safe container, uncovered. Microwave for 3-4 minutes.

Stir.

Let sit until the jelly has cooled completely.

Tip: This makes a very messy treat! Try serving it in a container on a washable floor surface for easy cleanup.

Yummy!
This is great served as a complement to the oatmeal recipe on page 34.

Illustration from *The Guinea Pigs' Summer Storybook.*

PICNIC CHIPS

2 tablespoons pellets
2 tablespoons oats
1/4 cup water

Preheat oven to 350 degrees.

Whirl the pellets and oats in a blender until they obtain a flour-like texture. Combine this with water in a bowl, and mix together.

Drop by the spoonful onto a cookie tray. Flatten into 7 "chips."

Bake 15 minutes.

Allow to cool on the tray.

Illustration from *The Guinea Pigs' Summer Storybook*.

Carrot Chips

1 carrot, *or* 5-7 baby-cut carrots

Preheat oven to 375 degrees.

Slice carrot(s) into thin, chip-shaped pieces. Place the pieces flat on a cookie sheet, separated from one another.

Bake for 10 minutes.

Let the chips cool completely on the cookie sheet.

~

For small animals, guinea pigs are packed with personality. And that personality really comes out when they want a treat!

~

SLUMBER PARTY STAND-BYs

Pizza and Popcorn, Comin' Up!

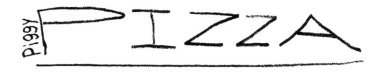

Crust
1/4 cup cornmeal
1/4 cup water

Preheat oven to 350 degrees. Combine the ingredients in a bowl. Let sit for 10 minutes. Drain off the extra water.

Pour the mixture in a circle shape on the center of a cookie sheet.

Bake for 10 minutes. Cool completely on the sheet.

Sauce
1/4 cup diced carrots.

Whirl the carrots in a blender. Using a

knife, spread the "sauce" on the pizza crust. (You can add more water for desired consistency.)

<u>Toppings</u>
Sliced carrots, food pellets, apples . . .

Cut into slices, or serve whole! This pizza serves a whole party of pigs.

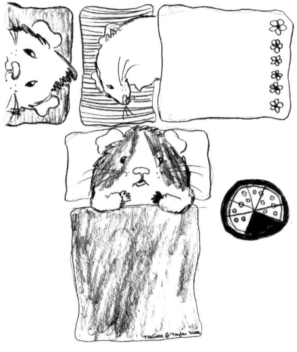

Illustration from *The Guinea Pigs' Summer Storybook.*

Piggy POPCORN

~ This popcorn is salt-free, oil-free, and butter-free! ~

1 teaspoon honey
1 teaspoon popcorn (old-fashioned)

Put honey and popcorn in a microwave-save container with a lid that "vents" air. Coat each kernel in the honey. Put on the lid.

Microwave for approximately 1 1/2 minutes. Let cool completely before serving.

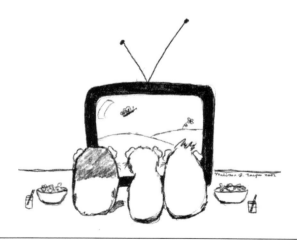

Illustration from *The Guinea Pigs' Summer Storybook*.

CHERRY CANDY

5 cherries

Set oven to 375 degrees.

Cut cherries in half, and remove the pits. Lay gooey-side up on a cookie sheet.

Bake for 20 minutes. Let them cool completely on the tray.

This makes 10 cherry "candies" that are a tad less messy than eating them uncooked. Remember to always let treats cool to room temperature before serving them.

GRAPE GUMDROPS

5 grapes
1 teaspoon pellets

Preheat the oven to 350 degrees.

Cut the grapes in half the short way,

making gumdrop shapes.

Blend the pellets in a blender. Dip the cut side of each grape half into this powder.

Place the grapes on their sides on a cookie sheet.

Bake for 5 minutes. Cool completely before serving.

Illustration from *The Guinea Pigs' Fall Storybook.*

Super Juice

7 baby-cut carrots
7 baby-sized tomatoes
1 4-5" stalk celery
1 dose Vitamin C supplement (optional)
1 cup water

Blend carrots, tomatoes, celery, and supplement lightly in a blender.

Pour the ingredients into a bowl. Add water. Let it sit/soak for about 45 minutes.

Use a strainer to separate the juice from the pulp.

This serves a whole crew of super pigs!

~
To get your guinea pig to wheeek *for treats, try rustling bags before giving him something like hay or a carrot. He'll quickly associate the sound of the bag with getting something good.*
~

CAVY

For each kabob, you will need:

1 piece Timothy hay
2-4 carrot slices (baby-cut work best)
O-shaped, natural cereal (3-4 pieces)

Select a thick, strong piece of Timothy hay. It doesn't need to be long—short is better.

Use a toothpick to make a hole in the middle of each carrot slice. Slide 1-2 carrot slices onto the Timothy hay (they should just fit). Next, slide on a few pieces of cereal.

End the kabob with 1-2 more carrot slices.

These are adorable, easy to make, and guinea pigs just love them! Try experimenting with other food additions to the kabob. You can poke holes in other small foods by using a toothpick.

~

Teach your guinea pig how to "stand" for treats. It's easy! Once she's tame enough to take food from your hand, begin putting it higher so that she must stretch to get it. Continue on with this over time, until she must lift her front legs in order to reach and obtain the treat.

~

Illustration from *The Guinea Pigs' Spring Storybook.*

LAYERED SALAD

You'll need only small quantities of each of the following ingredients:

Romaine lettuce
Cucumber
Celery leaves
Yellow summer squash
No-Chew Yummy Glue (page 36)
Picnic Chips (page 12)
Carrots

In a non-tip bowl, shred a bit of lettuce. Add a couple slices of cucumber on top, to resemble onions. Next, add celery leaves, to resemble spinach. Cut slices of squash from the small end. Add these to look like eggs. If you'd like, add No-Chew Yummy Glue—it is your "mayonnaise." You can crumble part of a Picnic Chip into the salad to resemble little pieces of bacon.

Last of all, grate a carrot over the top, to resemble cheese.

CORN DOGS

4 baby-cut carrots (choose the smallest)
4 sturdy, very green pieces of Timothy hay
1/4 cup cornmeal
1/4 cup water

Preheat the oven to 350 degrees.

Use a toothpick to make a hole in one end of each carrot. Slide in a piece of hay in that end.

Combine the cornmeal and water. Mix. Let sit for 10 minutes. Stir again, then drain off any extra "puddle" of water.

Form small sections of dough into 4 oblong shapes on a cookie sheet. Place a carrot on top, then cover the carrot with more dough.

Bake for 10 minutes.

Allow the corn dogs to cool on the sheet before removing them. If the dough crumbles off, you can reform it back on.

These are a big hit as a treat. They're messy and fun!

~

Does your guinea pig need to work off some of his tub? Use a large, short cardboard box as the base for a simple maze. Use masking tape and other pieces of cardboard to form the interior. Place a treat at the end.

~

Illustration from *The Guinea Pigs' Summer Storybook.*

Chewy BANANA CHIPS

1 ripe banana

Preheat the oven to 350 degrees.

Remove the peel from the banana. Slice the banana into chip shapes.

Place each piece flat on a cookie sheet. Bake for 8-10 minutes on each side. Let the chips cool in between baking each side, and after baking.

·COLESLAW·

1 tablespoon carrots
1 tablespoon celery leaves
1 tablespoon oats
1 tablespoon water
1 teaspoon raisins

Place all of the fixings, except the raisins, into a blender. Blend until the mixture obtains a consistency that is similar to coleslaw.

Remove mix from the blender, and stir in the raisins.

Serve in a bowl.

Illustration from *The Guinea Pigs' Winter Storybook*

Blueberry Crumble Cake

1/4 cup cornmeal
1/4 cup water
3 tablespoons blueberries

Combine the cornmeal and water in a blender.

Pour the mixture into a microwave-safe bowl and stir in the blueberries. Microwave, uncovered, for 1 1/2 minutes.

Carefully remove the bowl (it's hot!) and put the mixture in a non-tip bowl. Let the crumble cake cool thoroughly before serving.

Illustration from *The Guinea Pigs' Fall Storybook*.

Oatmeal Cookies

1 banana
1/2 cup instant oats
1 tablespoon water
1 tablespoon raisins

Preheat the oven to 350 degrees.

Remove and discard the banana peel. Cream the banana in a blender.

Pour the banana cream into a bowl. Stir in the oats. Add water. Mix. Add raisins. Stir.

Drop by the tablespoonful onto a cookie sheet. Reshape slightly if desired.

Bake the cookies for 12 minutes.

Let the cookies cool completely on the cookie sheet before removing them.

Makes half a dozen oatmeal cookies.

Piggybilli

5 cherry-sized tomatoes
4" stalk of celery
1 teaspoon corn

Put the tomatoes and celery in a blender, and whirl until they are slightly chopped.

Put in a non-tip bowl, and stir in the corn.

Illustration from *The Guinea Pigs' Fall Storybook*.

30

Carrot Punch

7 baby-cut carrots, *or* 1/4 cup
   diced carrots
1/2 cup water

Whirl the carrots and water in a blender, until the carrots are completely liquefied.
   This serves a whole piggy party!

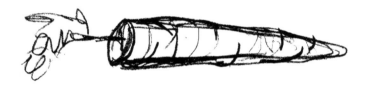

~

Try feeding your guinea pig a treat at the same time each day. She will learn to expect the treat at that time, and you'll be sure to be greeted with a lot of excitement— like running around, wheeeking, *or begging!*

~

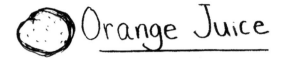 # Orange Juice

1 orange

Roll the orange on a table for 1-2 minutes, pressing down with the palm of your hand. Cut the orange in half. Squeeze each half into a non-tip bowl, removing seeds.

Illustration from *The Guinea Pigs' Summer Storybook.*

Couch-cavy Cookies

1/2 cup guinea pig pellets
1 tablespoon guinea pig-safe seed treat mix
1/2 cup water

Preheat oven to 350 degrees.

Whirl the pellets in a *dry* blender. The blender must be dry, because this will make a "flour" base. In a bowl, combine all the ingredients and stir thoroughly.

Drop by tablespoonful on a cookie sheet, making 10 cookies. Place the cookie sheet in the oven and bake for 15 minutes. Allow the cookies to cool before removing them.

~

Guinea pigs can live to be eight years old, or even older! One of mine lived to be almost nine. Encourage them not to be couch potatoes, with daily play sessions!

~

Illustration from *The Guinea Pigs' Summer Storybook*.

OATMEAL

2 tablespoons oats (instant* or old-
  fashioned)
3 tablespoons water

Put the ingredients in a microwave-safe
container and microwave for approximately a minute. Stir well.
  Store in the fridge until well cooled, and
then serve to your guinea pig(s).
  Remove uneaten portion—it's messy!

Variations

After microwaving, add small pieces of an
apple or carrot. Or, make fruity oatmeal by
using the jelly on page 10.

* Instant oats will be thicker, so you may
wish to use more water, though it's not
necessary.

~

A cardboard oatmeal container makes the most wonderful of toys! Cut out the closed end so that it forms a tube.

~

Oat Flavor

Blend a small amount of oats in a blender.

In a bowl, combine this "oat flour" with water, until it obtains a paste-like texture.

Guinea pigs enjoy sampling this sticky treat off a spoon! Be sure to provide plenty of water to help wash it down.

Wheat Flavor

Follow the instructions in the recipe above, but substitute normal flour for oats. You won't need to blend the wheat before beginning.

~ This was the first recipe I invented for guinea pigs, back when I was a little girl. ~

Illustration from *The Guinea Pigs' Winter Storybook.*

Sweet & Sour

Record Cookies

Featuring your favorite classics:
* ***Orange*** *You Lovely, Cavy Baby*
* *My Sweet **Honey** Guinea*
* *You **Oat** to Be Mine*
* *You're Such a **Pellet** is Wonderful*

1/2 orange (remove the peel and seeds)
1 tablespoon honey
2 tablespoons oats
3 tablespoons pellets

Preheat the oven to 350 degrees.

Combine all the ingredients in a blender.

Put the dough by tablespoonful on a cookie sheet, making 6 cookies. Bake for 13-15 minutes.

Let the cookies cool completely on the cookie sheet.

*Young and old alike can enjoy the
friendship of a guinea pig!*

~

Illustration from *The Guinea Pigs' Fall Storybook.*

SOUPS

FRUIT SOUP

1 orange slice
1/8 portion of an apple
3 tablespoons water

Blend all ingredients together in a blender. Pour into a non-tip bowl and serve.

These fruits are available year-round. At other times of the year, try safe seasonal fruits for a different flavor.

~

Cavies have a small sound-based language that we can actually learn to understand!

~

CORN CHOWDER

1 tablespoon sweet corn
2 tablespoons water

Blend corn and water together in a blender.
Serve in a non-tip bowl.

Birthday Cake

Cavy Cake tin (see below)
1/2 an apple
3 baby-cut carrots
1/2 cup oats
4 tablespoons water

Cavy Cake Tin

First, let's make a guinea pig birthday cake tin. It's something you can keep and reuse!

Find a can/tin at the store that holds a canned food item, like pineapple rings. It should measure 2" high by 3 1/2" in diameter. Open it up, and thoroughly clean it out. Now, you have a cake tin!

Cake

Set the oven at 350 degrees.

Chop the apple and carrots in a blender. Put into a bowl and add the oats. Mix. Add water by the tablespoon, stirring thoroughly.

Put the batter in the tin, and bake the cake for 20-25 minutes. Serves a piggy party!

Optional Additions
* Frost the cake with No-Chew Yummy Glue (page 36).
* Top with baby-cut carrots to look like candles. One for each year!

Illustration from *The Guinea Pigs' Summer Storybook.*

Apple Bundle Truffles

1 apple, peeled and cored
Oats

Preheat oven to 350 degrees.

Blend the apple in a blender until its pieces are about the size of oats.

Place apple pieces in a microwave-safe container and microwave for 20 seconds.

Spread aluminum foil on a cookie sheet, and place apple on the sheet by the spoonful, making about 8 groupings. Be sure to compact the apple pieces together.

Bake for 15 minutes.

Let the apple bundle pieces cool completely on the foil before removing them.

Place some oats in a bowl. Take an apple mix and form it into a ball. Roll the ball in the oats.

~

Guinea pigs give a lot back to their owners, through their devotion and friendship.

~

And now we present . . .

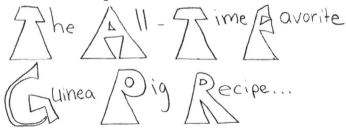

The All-Time Favorite Guinea Pig Recipe...

1 carrot

Take a carrot. Wash it thoroughly.
Serve quickly. Hurry! Hurry!

Index

Beverages
Carrot Punch   .   .   .   31
Orange Juice   .   .   .   32
Super Juice   .   .   .   19

Cakes and Cookies
Birthday Cake   .   .   .   42
Blueberry Crumble Cake   .   28
Couch-cavy Cookies   .   .   33
Oatmeal Cookies .   .   .   29
Sweet and Sour Record Cookies   38

Cereals
No-Chew Yummy Glue .   .   36
Oatmeal   34

Chips and Popcorn
Carrot Chips   .   .   .   13
Chewy Banana Chips   .   .   26
Picnic Chips   .   .   .   12
Piggy Popcorn   .   .   .   16

Desserts
Apple Bundle Truffles .   .   45
Cherry Candy   .   .   .   17
Grape Gumdrops .   .   .   17

Main Dishes

Cavy Cabobs . . . 20
Corn Dogs 24
Piggy Pizza 14

Salads and Relishes

Cherry-Apple Jelly . . 10
Coleslaw 27
Layered Salad . . . 23
Mini Guinea . . . 8
Piggylilli 30

Soups

Corn Chowder . . . 41
Fruit Soup 40

The All-Time Favorite Guinea Pig Recipe

. 46

The index categories are just for fun. The recipes are all treats, and only to be fed to guinea pigs in tiny amounts.

Tips for Treats

Creative Cookies

Instead of making cookies in the large shapes recommended, you can try making them small and piggy-sized. Or, make shapes! Adjust the baking duration to accommodate any changes you make.

Tasty Traditions

Create traditions with treats. For example, the Birthday Cake (see page 42) is fun to give to your cavy every year.

Teaching Trust

Regularly offer a treat to a shy guinea pig, even if he won't take it. Wait a bit, then set it down near him if he won't accept it. You can do this while holding him, and when he's in his enclosure. Even though he may not respond to your offers of a treat at first, he'll learn to associate you with good things.

Tricks for Treats

Teach your guinea pig to exercise for her treats. She can learn how to beg on her hind legs (see page 21), or get to the end of a maze (see page 25). You'll have fun, bond, and she'll work off some calories!

About the author and taste testers

Melissa J. Taylor got her first guinea pig when she was nine years old. Melissa's original taste testers for this cookbook were (from left to right) Muffy, Henna, and Roo.

Muffy and Henna are also characters in The Guinea Pigs' Storybook series, which follows eight guinea pig friends through a year of adventures.

29333102R00032

Printed in Great Britain
by Amazon